MW00744529

Best Wishes

uncle Ken

"The Other Way"
(The Grass Roots Way)
To
Socio-Economic Survival for Man and the Environment.

This is the way which we have never tried in our quest to reach the Ultimate Goal of a
Debt - free,
Well-nourished, Poverty-free, World Society.

When compatibly allied with the world of Nature, "**This Other Way**" could lead to a world-wide social environment
of
Peace, Harmony, Simplicity,
Equal Opportunity and Wellbeing
For all of us.

Try this

"Anodyne for the world's ills"
-Administered by-

Author

Copyright © 2003 by Kenneth E. Muma

ISBN 0-7414-1269-1

Published by:

PUBLISHING.COM

519 West Lancaster Avenue
Haverford, PA 19041-1413
Info@buybooksontheweb.com
www.buybooksontheweb.com
Toll-free (877) BUY BOOK
Local Phone (610) 520-2500
Fax (610) 519-0261

Printed in the United States of America

Printed on Recycled Paper

Published January, 2003

Table of Contents

*This book was Written and Dedicated
To the Loving Memory of*

Mary,

*my late wife and mother of my little family. I also dedicate
this book to my late parents John and Mary Muma and their
family on the little farm where I was born and raised.*

*This book is further dedicated to the thousands of de-
voted men and women of all nationalities, colours and creeds
the world over, who have given and continue to give of their
lives and their talents in order to physically and spiritually
assist those who are less fortunate.*

*This treatise is written for all those Friends and Students
of Nature and those who believe in their interdependent relationship to Mother Nature as well as to the "Supreme Creator" of all life, knowing that it was this "Creator" who had
cast them into their unique role.*

*I do not forget all of those who are concerned about the
inherent right of every person to the entitlement of an equal
portion of this planet's **natural** as well as **recreated** wealth.*

*I am also mindful of those Scientists and Philosophers, as
well as Social Workers who have and still are paving the
way for a more closely knit society. Then there are those
who yearn for a simpler life, with all of those basic require-
ments for Health and Wellbeing for everyone.*

Preface

The Old Way

This is the "Known Way". It is now quite worn out. It is rough and broken and no longer safe for use. This way causes many unwarranted accidents and sufferings for the Human Race. This "Known Way" is the way of "Free Enterprise" and "Big Business". It carries our "Life Traveller" along the rocky road of "Competitive Capitalism" down to the sea of "Rampant Consumerism", where the once beautiful shores are now piled high with pollution-forming trash and garbage. Here, the traveller meets the ever-present struggle to survive the destructive waves of recurring Wars and Insidious Terrorism, which are vainly being countered by the ages-old, fallacious policy of rendering, "An eye for an eye". Finally, when we come to the end of the road, we see there are no more "Eyes" to give. The result is ***Total Blackout!***

"The Other Way"

This is a new way, having each of its Component parts thoroughly tested for Reliability, Strength and Endurance. May the serious, thoughtful reader carefully peruse each thought-filled phrase, so that he or she may clearly find his or her way and so enjoy travelling with this Philosopher of "The Back Forty"!

To all of those wanderers who have lost their way in this "welter" we call Civilization, it is the hope that the "Other Way" will set them on the right course to their goal *of Peace, Simplicity, Security and Health.*

It is the belief of this author that the course that we have been following for the past many millenniums, has now brought us to a detour. Many conflicting signposts send us hither and yon in our quest to find the best way out of our dilemma and so point us on our way to our destination. This leads the author to believe that now is the time for the human family to learn about "The Other Way."

It is apparent that the base which now shakily supports our Civilization has begun to crumble. It is evident that it will no longer safely support our rapidly growing population's many diversified demands for a place where each of us can Live, Love, Play and Share with one another according to each individual's needs, while at the same time, recognizing the "Sanctity of all life".

Within these pages, I invite you to read and study this "Grass Roots Way" to real freedom with security. This 'way' is a "Care and Share", Cashless Economy 'Way'. In this environment, "Industry" would have abandoned its responsibilities to "Business", making it possible to then serve Humanity as a real "Free Enterprise". This treatise maps out "The Other Way" as it is recounted to you, a Neighbour, who might just be passing by the cabin door of my alias, *Timothy Haystubble*.

Who is this Character From
"The Back Forty"?

Meet my Alias!

I expect it is well known that 'Timothy Grass' is perhaps one of the more common of the natural feed crops grown for the feeding of livestock, at least by some of the less prosperous farmers in my neck of the woods. This crop usually grows naturally, in association with such common weed plants as wild mustard, sow thistle, Canada thistle, milkweed, wild daisy, goldenrod, dandelions and many more.

The hay stubble is the part of the plant left in the field after the crop has been taken off, either by modern mowing machinery or by the more primitive method employing the two-handed scythe. Although this stubble may, to some casual observer appear quite useless, it is either ploughed under to provide mulch for other crops, or just left to lie dormant to become next season's hay crop.

The "Back Forty" derives from that smallish, insignificant tract of land away at the back of the farm. This bit of land is considered of little value and so, often gets neglected. Consequently, Nature soon takes over, forming a habitat for all sorts of these so called weeds. These plants are necessary elements of Nature, attracting butterflies, bees and other insects. Many wild shrubs and young trees have become suitable habitats for song birds, woodchucks, rabbits and chipmunks. Here Nature holds sway producing a human sanctuary of relative peace and quiet, seemingly far removed from the hustle and bustle, the stress and clatter of modern Civilization.

Putting all of these elements together, one arrives at the phrase which suggested the name of my - 'Alias' –

Timothy Haystubble,
Hailing from the Back Forty.

-1-

My Thesis Really Begins Here.

So now, I will let **"Timothy Haystubble"** take over and tell you
All about this concept of
New Wine Skins
For
New Wine

"Howdy Neighbour!

"Come on over, sit a spell and 'make yourself to home',
as they used to say.

"I am sorry that the best I have to offer for refreshment
this afternoon is this pitcher of fresh, sweet Apple Cider.
However if you feel the need for more, just let me know.
There's a lot more where this came from!

"See that apple tree yonder?

"Well siree, the fruit from that tree makes the best sweet
apple cider anywhere around! At least that's what my neighbours say.

"You know, when I sit here on my front steps, thinking
and whittling, whittling and thinking, as I quite often do, I
look back over the events of the past century with wonder—

"The more I think about it, the more it seems to me quite
evident, that our patient, much abused, old planet has gone
through a lot of very momentous changes, both physical and
social.

"For example: I have noticed that our Sciences and our
Technologies, controlled and manipulated, as they seem to
be, solely by Business Interests, both large and small, have
very radically changed our way of life - yours and mine.

1

"The results of some of these changes seem to be for the better, especially for a certain privileged minority. Those folks who were fortunate to have started off with plenty were enabled to obtain what seemed to be even more than their share. However, on the other hand, those who had very little to start with, often lost all that they had struggled a lifetime of uncertainty to achieve. Now just take Peter Brown. His place has just been taken over by the bank. It seems that he got behind in his mortgage payment. The banking authorities foreclosed and took over his farm without thought for the wellbeing of him or his family.

"Following the 'Great Depression of the Thirties', which was one of the economic side-effects resulting from the 'First World War', we all experienced that devastating scourge of the 'Second World War', which as you recall, was Adolf Hitler's arrogant, though vain, attempt to rule the world. This crisis provided the rest of the world with a second chance to put an end to all future wars. What a foolish thought it was to think that 'Peace' could be won as a prize for the mass killing of other human beings, as well as causing the destruction of vast amounts of natural and man-made products!

"In spite of the sincere efforts of certain well-meaning organizations, (including the League of Nations, followed by the United Nations, as well as many others), to obtain lasting peace for all people, it is seen that these attempts brought only temporary relief from our economic and social distress.

"As of now, there is no assurance of ever obtaining world peace by following the way of the 'Status Quo', supported as it seems necessary, by military might - 'the way of the sword'.

"With the onset of that 'Second World War', many young men and women were persuaded to enlist as front-line fighting soldiers, all in the name of 'defending their Country'. Those who could not be gently persuaded to 'join up', were conscripted. It was thought, everyone must do his or her patriotic duty in the service of his or her native land, by standing up and marching to kill or be killed by other men

2

(the enemy). They too, the enemy, had been carefully trained to operate their life-destroying machines. Let those who shoot first, with the most up-to-date equipment be declared the winners! This it seems is the first 'law of battle'.

"The alternative form of duty was to *faithfully* help by serving those essential industries at home some of which had been tooled to produce the instruments of war, as well as others for food, clothing, etc, for all fellow humans. We were all in this colossal devastation together, with those human beings who robotically operated the technologies to produce those weapons of modern warfare.

"With this second all-out war, we thought that we had saved our world from destruction as well as from domination by the Nazi Super Power. At the same time, did we not acquiesce to the killing of millions of human beings, soldiers and civilians alike, of any age, without regard for their nationality or religion, all in the name of Peace and National Security? Just to make sure that this job had been done well, were we not complacent in the development and the deployment of two Atomic Bombs, thereby making ourselves accountable for many more innocent civilians along with their homes and private property?

"Thus we ushered in the dangerous and uncertain 'Atomic Age'. To show our superiority we allowed the munitions makers to make and stock-pile many thousands of new, improved nuclear war-heads, which we now have outlawed and do not know how to get rid of.

"My friend, conflicts have never been solved by fighting and killing. They never will be!

"Just like the fable of the 'Magic Broomstick'. This broomstick, when broken into many pieces, was no longer one broomstick. It became many little broomsticks-fragments of the original one. Wars within and between nations have continued to harass humanity and to ravage the world.

"This new 'salvation for our way of life', has again taken us on a campaign, whose ultimate goal could very well be the destruction of our environment along with the destruction of our society and ultimately the end of the Human Race— Well this is the way it looks to me!

"This *Competitive Spirit,* which was born and found to be very useful during humanity's primitive years, has now been released and well-nurtured in order to rebuild our economy to a place of pre-eminence among the wealthy nations of the world.

"Today, many of us ordinary folk are struggling to just stay alive in this increasingly hyperactive, free enterprise, competitive, capitalist society.

"This competitive spirit is called 'very good' by those who have plenty as well as by the over-persuasive media, which in turn, are sponsored by this ruling 'competitive system'. It seems important in this 'game of life', to at least beat the other guy in order to get ahead and be first. These two, *Security* and *Success,* are held up as the 'Grand Prizes' for winning, in this competitive, Free Enterprise Society.

"'Industries' paired with and controlled by *'Businesses'* are encouraged to *make profit and production, their goal.* We of the general public also, are carefully taught to believe that it is quite all right to make as much profit from as much production as possible on every transaction. The devastating results of all this is the over-use and waste of our natural resources, whether they are renewable or not. As a result, this produces an increase in the disastrous, noxious, life-destroying world pollution of many types. Now our civilized world has all but conquered Nature and has bid her to bend and sway to this seductive tune of *Greed and Profit.*

"Well as I have said, we have just emerged from the 20th century and are starting the 3rd millennium. Many religious leaders as well as Business and Banking Institutions, using the tools of Technology and installed Industries are making many and varied predictions regarding this *'New Era'*. Be assured my friend, these predictions, will in no small way affect our Ecology and our Social life as well as the Health and wellbeing of each of us. For this reason we must be very careful for what we are asking!"

-2-

New Wine Skins for New Wine

"My friend, I see your drink is quite finished. Ha, Ha, Ha! There must be a hole in the bottom of that mug which I gave you.

"Let me give you a fill up of some more of this delicious sweet apple cider!

"While you are sipping your cider, allow me to tell you about my latest invention, which I have chosen to call

'New wine skins for new wine'.

"A thought came to me while I was sitting here thinking about all of that distressing news coming in on my little radio. With all our brilliant scientists and engineers, all of our astute politicians and economists as well as all of our prosperous business-controlled industrial organizations, why is it that we have not yet learned how to distribute all of those goods and services, which we have learned how to produce in sufficient abundance, to satisfy each person's needs when and where they're needed? Is it that most of the world's social problems are due to the fact that we keep on trying to store 'new wine in old wine skins'? We should just think about this for awhile.

"By golly, I said to myself that must be the answer. We should select new 'Wine Skins' for our 'New Wine'! We should choose a shoe that fits the wearer for size and shape. All of these thoughts came to me in my meditation right here on my front steps, here on my 'Back Forty'. That's right!

"The world has been producing a lot of 'New Wine' for some time now. Because it seemed more economical, in the short run, to use the old bottles over and over again, this is what we have been doing. This saved money alright, but it produced a lot of spilled wine from many broken bottles to boot. These broken bottles and spilled wine produced a great waste of our natural resources and at the same time has produced a considerable amount of pollution, which is proving dangerous to man, plants and animals.

"The **'New Wine'** stands for the rapid development in *Science* along with its companion *Technology* as applied to the service of humanity. 'Wine Skins' refers to the outmoded methods, which the world has continuously used in trying to solve World Social problems, nationally and internationally.

"This new **'Wine Skin'** represents a proposed method for making sure that each person would benefit by all of these discoveries and inventions which are designed not only to save lives but also to assist folks in getting along with other folks. For these reasons I thought it quite fitting that this idea should be made available as well as understandable for the use of all of mankind as well as the environment. Such an idea would not be for sale as a consumable commodity, but would be freely available to everyone, all nationalities, all races, male and female.

"Now just listen while I tell you what my invention could do for all of us:

"First of all it could be very helpful in rescuing our Planet Earth from its abuse and eminent destruction, which has been largely generated by the ruthless machinations of 20th century mankind.

"Furthermore, this invention could be employed to help feed the starving, clothe the naked, shelter the homeless, heal the sick, join Nation to Nation by eliminating National boundaries, mend broken relationships, tame the lions and aid in bringing about Peace and Fellowship among all people.

"With this invention, used in co-operation with Science and modern Technology, many of the arid lands could be induced to produce food and other natural products when and if needed. In time, many of our forgotten streams would begin to flow with 'life-giving water' once more.

"With this invention we could take the time to gaze up into the night sky and view the stars and moon with wonder.

6

We would then have just cause to marvel at the immensity and mystery of the Creator's handiwork.

"Well Neighbour, I suggest that now is the time for the world to light a *New Candle* and get a clean sheet of environment friendly, recycled parchment. Now is the time to think new thoughts and to formulate new plans. Now is the time to seriously think about this invention, which I am about to disclose to you. Without new wine skins, I believe there is real danger that the 'New Wine' of the 21st Century could become sour, bitter and contaminated with the poisons of Mad Scientists and self-seeking Politicians. This contaminated new wine would no doubt produce a beverage, the consumption of which would make Fools, Mad Men and Women of the rest of us."

-3-

The Concern of the Devas

"Near the close of the day, I often wander to the foot of yonder maple tree, the one on the edge of my wood lot. There in the quiet of Nature, I can rest a spell and (while resting), reflect on the news of the day - how National and world events are affecting our society. This is where the 'Still Small Voice' speaks to me. This is where the 'Devas of Nature' whisper their wisdom for all those who will care to listen.

"It has been said: 'those who have ears to hear let them hear' and learn what Nature has to say.

"These little 'Devas' (Divine, benevolent Nature Spirits) are justifiably concerned about our many friends in their Nature realm - our wood lots, our wet lands, our swamps, our rivers and our lakes.

"These 'Devas' are worried about the disappearance of many of those vital creatures making up what we call our 'wild life'. All of these are essential parts of our own lives. All life comes from one source and is therefore related and interdependent.

"They are concerned about our bird neighbours as well as the insects, on which these bird neighbours feed.

"They tell me that they are troubled by the rapid disappearance of our life-giving topsoil as well as the pollution of the soil that is left. They know that rich, clean, lively topsoil is very essential for growing all of the vital, life-giving food, which is so necessary for the survival of all herbivorous creatures, including man.

"They are concerned about the diminishing supply of unpolluted fresh water, which is a vital factor for all life on our planet. These friendly, helpful 'Nature Spirits' are trying to warn us of the fact that Humanity, world-wide, must immediately take the necessary steps to do the corrective things necessary to save our environment.

"The authorities have talked about certain future plans of action for a very long time. It is high time that they got busy and did something constructive, before it is too late. That is the gist of what they told me, my friend.

"This sort of constructive action would undoubtedly mean the necessity to change some of our most cherished concepts and attitudes as well as some of our old notions about 'Life'. It is important that we stop now, turn around if necessary, and go '*the Other Way*'.

"They also reminded me that it is very unwise to put '*New Wine*' into '*Old Wine Skins*'. Of course I agree with them completely. We do need a '*New Wine*', if a change for the better is to be made in this new millennium. For this reason, it seemed expedient that someone must design and detail the plans for '*New Wine Skins*' to contain this '*New Wine*'.

"Well this sort of set me to thinking about the matter! Maybe, in due time, I would find the answer; so I will keep the way clear for this right answer to come to me. I must keep on thinking!"

-4-

Working with Nature

"Well, you know Neighbour, I believe it is advisable that we all learn to understand and interpret this 'Drama of Life', in which we are each playing a part. It is also necessary that we learn to play this part in 'Co-operation', not in 'Competition' with the other members of the cast. This is necessary if we wish to receive the applause of approval from our 'Director'. We must also learn that this part we are assigned to play must fit in with each of the other parts. We must accept the universal fact that each unit of 'Nature' also plays a part in this 'Drama'.

"For this reason, each of these little units of Nature must be given its due respect, as well as an opportunity to fill its allotted role. Many of us have gotten so far away from Nature and its elemental forces that I am afraid we have forgotten the importance of the essential things that Nature, not only has done, but is continually doing for our wellbeing.

"Quite often, many businesses, large and small, seem to believe that Nature sometimes stands in the way of their progress and their profit. They unthinkingly assume that these offending elements of nature need to be eliminated. As a result of this error in thinking, much of Nature's bounty and beauty have been irreplaceably destroyed. In retaliation, it seems that Nature has, at times, visited us with plagues of floods, fires, tornadoes, hurricanes, droughts and famines.

"As I have said, I believe that many of us have gotten so far removed from the real feel of Nature that we do not fully realize the amount of power that these natural elements display when applied against our own puny efforts which we call 'Progress'. However, our Scientists and Engineers have learned a great deal about the Natural laws of the universe.

Where and when profitable for Business, these corporate scientists and engineers have manifested much of this knowledge for the benefit and pleasure of those who can afford to acquire this manifestation in the form of *Goods and Services*."

-5-

Control of Science and Technology

"They tell me that it took our very ancient ancestors quite a long time to learn to stand erect and walk properly on their own two flat feet. When once they got started, they found that they could get where they wanted to go more quickly by running. So it was, I expect, the 'Human Race' got started!

"Well sir, Humanity was in such a hurry to get on with this 'Human Race' that they had to contrive better and faster means of travel. This meant that 'roads' should be built by widening and improving those man-made trails through the forests and across the plains. Then as the needs arose, these had to be improved upon.

"Eventually creative Technology, financed by Business interests, invented and constructed motor vehicles. These were able to travel many times faster than the horse-drawn carts of those early days.

"These new vehicles required improved roads as well as 'bridges' to span rivers and ravines. In order to save time, rather than going around a mountain, it was found to be more expedient to bore a tunnel through the mountain. When someone got the idea that it would be wonderful as well as profitable, especially for the Military, to be able to fly like a bird, flying machines were successfully contrived and built – not just one or two but by the tens of thousands. These super aircraft soon took on the status of an Air Force, becoming an important adjunct to the 'military machine'.

"Finally, with science combined with Mankind's advanced technology, huge jet-propelled aircraft were constructed to speed the movement of passengers as well as

12

commerce. For many, in this high-speed business economy, speed goes hand in hand with profit and production, if we wish to win this race! It even seems to be quite all right to start before the 'starting gun'. This is called strategy and in most instances of practice, it is justified on the books of man-made law.

"However, the race is not over yet. Man's need and greed have not been satisfied by conquering Nature and her natural forces on Earth. There are billions of mysteries in the far-out reaches of infinite space and beyond. These unknown areas also need to be explored. The inhabitants, if any, need to be conquered and exploited to meet our demands. The moon has already felt the conqueror's footsteps! Mars is a tempting next milepost on our race. Billions of dollars are currently being spent by and for certain dedicated Scientists and Engineers working co-operatively around the world on a fantastic 'Space Station' idea. This is being spurred on by Business enterprises anxious to 'set up shop' on our neighbouring planet, Mars. Their goal is to eventually conquer space, with the hope of discovering intelligent life, although millions of light years from Earth, with whom they can never communicate or fraternize.

"Why is this necessary when there are several billions of human beings, here on Planet Earth, who even in the midst of plenty, are suffering, for the lack of food, clothing and shelter?

"At the same time, our highways are crowded with cars. Our city streets are jammed with traffic, making Safety a number one priority to Speed. (Speed and Safety are seldom able to 'sleep in the same bed'.) Our air is becoming polluted with more and more aircraft, thereby endangering the lives of our feathered friends, as well as over-using our life-giving oxygen.

"Nature's limited resources are rapidly being converted to Waste, Scrap and Pollution, producing insensitive Robotic Creatures out of Humanity here on Earth.

"The waterways are also becoming crowded and hazardous for man.

"Our experiences with the water environment began with primitive, thinking and reasoning mankind. The most elementary form of water vehicle was some primitive form of canoe. This probably began when some manlike creature discovered that a floating log was able to carry his or her weight, making it safe and easy to ride on the water for some distance. This was much better than swimming. These logs, in time, changed to dugouts, which took on many sizes and shapes. Then there were those distant relatives of our First Nations who discovered that even a large piece of tree bark was sufficient to carry at least one person on the surface of a lake or river. So it is probable that the now popular birch-bark and cedar canoes were born.

"From these beginnings came the rowboat, the sailboat, the steamship, the warship, the submarine and the nuclear powered water vehicles. Luxury passenger liners have now given rise to practical floating homes to allow coastal dwellers to safely accept the effects of 'climate change' and the resulting rise in the coastal waters.

"Please do not misunderstand me. I am not opposed to the development of Science and Technology when it is seen to be for the benefit of the whole development of Mankind. Our transportation technology along with our communication technology has been of great benefit to Mankind as well as to Nature."

-6-

To where is this Human Race Racing?

"The technology which has aided Man in his attempt to conquer 'Nature', both here and in space, is now apparently being used by certain 'insensitive elements' of humanity, called 'Big Business'. The wanton use of this Technology could unintentionally destroy man, the conqueror, along with his technology and his creations.

"In the twentieth century, these technological feats of mankind are, in reality the results of the co-operative efforts and ingenuity of a number of men and women using the raw material provided by Nature. This has been aided by the insatiable drive of 'Big Businesses' hoping to be the biggest and the best in their fields of operation.

"Is this the way that the universal race for supremacy is usually run? At any rate it seems so!

"This was further explained by the 'Deva of Industry' who whispered to me above the whirr and clatter of many noisy industrial operations. This Deva confided in me that the propelling force of 'Business' is that one universal idea, which we have learned to call *'The Money Price System'*.

"As we all know, this system uses a commodity called 'money tokens' or 'credit cards' in order to make possible the distribution of all of those mechanical and electrical devices, which right now are not only shaping and ruling but, to a large extent, *ruining our world*."

-7-

"The Money Price System"

"This 'Money Price System' was the invention of mankind. Unfortunately the inventor's progeny have allowed it to be developed to favour that certain minority, who were born with the unique genetic inheritance which would permit them to claim superiority over their neighbour. Today this 'Money price system' in our civilization, has assumed the role of a 'god'. It claims the place of leadership in almost all of our activities. Let me assure you friend and all of your neighbours, *this 'Money Price System' is not 'divine'*, as our ruling minority claim it to be. This very fault-ridden system can be replaced if we, the members of the human race, would now use our ingenuity to devise a different and better system.

"It is well to consider the place that money has assumed in modern society. For example, it is not even possible to obtain our essential food without the help of at least someone's money, cash or credit. Our homes, equipped with the essential furniture and other life and labour-saving devices are not obtainable without money. The clothes we wear are impossible to acquire without money of some sort. Our transportation, unless we choose to walk, has to be paid for in Cash or Credit. The electric power we use so freely in our homes is produced and distributed from 'Nature's limitless bounty of Energy', using the help of money of some sort. Businesses and Industries, including the often, elaborate buildings required to house them, have been built and paid for by cash or credit, including long-term mortgages, which we call stocks or bonds.

16

"Can you think of any thing or service we use today that has not been legally or illegally obtained by the use of 'Money'?

"On the other hand, one has but to observe the many adverse side effects that this complex system has had on society, and therefore on each individual in society.

"Consider the numerous wars being fought, occurring almost continuously, some between nations and some within nations. These destructive activities all require large sums of money or capital with which to buy the fighting equipment as well as the munitions required for their use. This is true of other resources that are appropriated and used destructively against societies everywhere.

"As is well known, wars are waged in order that one nation or a group within a nation can obtain superiority over some other nation; as well as between different groups within a nation. Invariably in war man destroys those things and those people whom he wishes to control. Much wealth, in the form of sophisticated weaponry as well as military and civilian lives and property is appropriated and destroyed to claim a war devastated country. The territory thus gained would then need to be repaired or rebuilt in order to restore its value. No one ever wins an armed conflict. Wars are all fought on the theory of an 'eye for an eye', which invariably expands to a 'tooth for a tooth' until both sides are rendered sightless and toothless. Being sightless, it is quite impossible for either side to see the other person's point of view. Being toothless, neither side can savour the ill-gotten fruits.

"Every day, numerous 'crimes' are committed, attempted or planned in order to obtain some of that necessary 'where-with-all', which is required in increasing amounts, to acquire the personal necessities for everyday living. Because of this lack of either 'Cash' or 'Credit', millions of men, women and children are forced to go without food, clothing and even shelter which are necessary to maintain health and life.

"In the getting of these things, which are essential for our health and welfare, do we ever take time to pause and reflect on the effects, good and bad that the 'Money System' has had in the development of our culture?

"I believe we usually tend to maximize the benefits and by doing so we justify the necessity for this 'money' system's operation. At the same time we tend to moralize that it was not the fault of the system, but rather our personal fault for having digressed from the economic principles necessary to allow it to work as we thought it should have worked for our particular purposes.

"To me it seems obvious that our civilization is in dire need for a new idea to *replace Money*. This new idea should be able to facilitate a just and equitable distribution of 'Goods and Services' (free from any harmful side effects), from the producer to the consumer. Economists, sometimes talk about a coming 'cashless society'. They are of course, referring to the growing popularity of the 'Visa idea', as well as the 'Bank debit card' systems. These however, are just other forms of 'Money' (deferred payment), and do not do anything to solve the need or the concern which I am presenting here."

"Now, I do hope that you will take time to think on those things, of which I have just told you!"

-8-

More about Life

"I believe that this world of ours could be correctly defined as an interconnection of all Life Forms plus all Life Forces. These life forms consist, not only of ourselves, whether white, black, brown, yellow or red, but also of all those other life forms, which we call Nature. All of these Life forms live and depend not only on each other, but also on the Life forces in the environment around them.

"In other words, 'Nature' is the manifestation of all of these elements, which are co-ordinated by the energy of some unfathomable *Power*, which I expect we will forever refer to as *'God'* - the nameless Being of our existence, our 'Consciousness.... the 'Awe' of our being.

"Back in the beginnings of time (it matters not when), it is probable that our natural environment was created in slow, planned stages. According to myth and legend, we were asked *to care for* and *to share with,* the other creatures of this world environment. In other words, mankind was commissioned to care for all of those *lesser life forms* as well as to care for each other in such a manner that they all might live together for their mutual Enjoyment as well as for their mutual Provision, *each one giving to the other so that the other also might live.*"

-9-

Sun, Wind and Rain

"Just feel that gentle, cooling breeze! It seems to speak to me with cautious words of wisdom. To me it says 'Look around you at Nature.' It is not at all like it was at the beginning of the 20th century. Much of our landscape has changed. 'Civilization' is encroaching on our Natural environment and claiming, in the name of 'Progress', much of Nature's prime territory.

Many virgin wood-lots have been raped to form pasture-lands, cornfields and wheat fields. Other wooded areas as well as many wetlands have been paved over to become city streets with parking lots to accommodate the increasing growth of passenger cars. Houses and factories have replaced many more of our wood-lots. Some streams, which should have matured as major freshwater sources for the use of humanity as well as Nature, have become stagnant and fouled with pollution originating from many indiscrete industrial as well as domestic operations. Other streams have just been allowed to dry up, along with all of their original life forms.

"This 'Breeze' can be very gentle when it is cooling our brows. It can also be very helpful in some of our industrial operations.

"Using our engineering skills, we have developed devices to harness these breezes to produce light and power to assist our everyday living. On the other hand, when these gentle breezes become hurricanes or tornadoes they can destroy all of those things that we have built.

"Therefore, at all times my friend, it is very important that we treat these air currents with both knowledge and respect.

"Those little 'Raindrops' splashing on the hard parched ground, have their own vitally important story to tell us. They remind us that, although they are a part of the fluid of all life, they are also capable of destroying it. We must respect them, and organize our activities to harmonize with their rhythms and their whimsies.

"When these little raindrops join forces with a host of other little raindrops, they can become a mighty force for good or for evil. On the one hand they can provide unlimited, pollution-free power to operate our Industries. They can provide light for our homes and our streets at night. On the other hand, when they are united in large bodies of water, as in flash floods, they can become a potential for great disaster and destruction.

"Therefore it is of great importance for us to keep our reservoirs, our streams, our rivers and our lakes free from hazardous, industrial waste. It is also advisable to keep our skies free from man-made toxic gases. In short, we should treat our water, from whatever source, as a precious commodity, to be cherished, conserved and when necessary shared but never sold or traded for profit.

"This trinity of elements is interdependent and co-related each depending on the other for its existence. We are required to learn, by trial and error perhaps, how to harness these energy sources for the beneficial uses of Humanity, leaving sufficient for the necessary uses of our Natural Environment.

"This entire Natural Environment, co-operating sustainably, is vital for the existence and survival of what we call 'Life', here on planet Earth."

-10-

'New Wine Skin'
(The secret revealed)

"My friend, the voices of Wisdom and Reason advise me that we, who understand these things, should go out into the world of People, civilized and otherwise. There as emissaries, we should co-work with our Neighbours, people of all Nations, Races, Gender, Age, Culture and Religion, as well as all of the Natural Elements and Forces around us. Our task is to add our assistance in designing and creating this *'New Wine Skin'*, which can properly and safely contain the *'New Wine'* for the present era as well as for the eras yet to come.

"I was advised that this *'New Wine Skin'* should be of a very simple nature, yet capable of doing its job efficiently and easily. It should be simple enough for the most untutored mind, with very little instruction, to be able to use it.

"With this criterion in mind, I mused for some time, and then the thought came to me as in a vision. What can be simpler than 'Asking'? We ask for things many times a day. In fact Industries perform their varied tasks throughout their operations using 'requisitions'-various signed slips of paper or punched cards, dispatched from person to person and from department to department. This led to the thought, why shouldn't all 'Industries' get together with their 'Scientists', 'Electronics Engineers' and 'Computer Technicians', who working in concert, develop the appropriate procedures to distribute their goods direct from their 'Industry' to the 'Consumer' without the restrictions imposed by this controlling concept which we know of as 'Business and Finance'.

"All of this could be made possible with the use of a special kind of electronic 'Requisition System', taking the form of a combination 'credit - debit card'. This in fact would

22

materialize as a special, new sort of card which I have chosen to call a *'Share Card'*.

"Following on this thought, why could not each industrial complex, whether designed for the production of Goods or Services, be solely responsible for the distribution of its output through suitable, special distribution centers or outlets more or less convenient to the consumer?

"This *'New Wine Skin'* would become the materialization, as well as the practical application of the ages-old philosophy, *'Caring and Sharing'*.

"Let us assume, as is now estimated, that the Earth's human population stands at some six billion people. Let us assume further, that each and every living person should be unconditionally entitled to a proportionate share of the wealth of the planet (one six billionth of the available products of Industry). To me this seems quite logical. "Each person would then be considered to be an equal shareholder as it were, of our Planet Earth, simply by virtue of being a member of *The Family of Man.*

"Now let us assume that an average size family is six people. This means that there would be about one billion family units living off and sharing the products of the earth.

This share could, more or less, be considered one's own private property, to use and care for wisely and kindly for ones own benefit as well as for the benefit of one's *Neighbour,* if and when such a Neighbour's need might arise.

"This is what *caring and sharing* is all about!

"Be assured however, if anyone claims more than one's proportionate share, then the Chain of Life would most surely be broken, requiring someone to have less or even none at all. This would be an unbalanced situation, which Nature abhors.

"Now that I have 'let the cat out of the bag', I am obliged to share the rest of the secrets of this invention with you and your neighbours. By doing this, it is to be hoped that this idea will not be kept a secret for very long!

"On this simple, yet practical Idea rests the security and life of our Civilization!

"In a practical sense, 'Sharing' would become as simple as 'Asking'. Ask and you shall receive in good honest measure, if and when the product or service becomes available.

"Most of the parts of this invention are already at hand. To complete the picture, all that would be required would be for electronics technicians to rearrange, co-ordinate and assemble these parts in the proper manner so as to produce this completed 'Wine Skin', as set forth in the several thoughts which I now confide in you.

"Having obtained the approval by a majority vote of the population, resulting from a series of National Referendums, a special world wide census would be held to register each and every individual. At this time of registration each person would be provided with a suitable, number-coded *'Share Card'*, which when signed would become one's unlimited purchasing power. This *'Share Card'* could also serve as the individual's ID card.

"At the birth of a child, the natural parents, or the authorized guardian would register the infant and be allotted its personal, *'Share Card'*. This card could be left in the care of the parents or guardian until this new child 'becomes of age' and able to act on its own.

"I should mention here that this new member of the human family would be born into a type of 'Society' (a real cashless society) which would have been given 'Public Ownership and Control' of all Lands and Natural Resources including those resources which are related to the production of Energy. Private, corporate or national ownership and control of any lands or resources, including real-estate, could not be allowed to exist anywhere in this new society. All of these belong to the 'General Public' for their development and legitimate uses, as needed. With the introduction of this 'Share Card', all forms of 'Money' would have become invalidated, world-wide, having no purchasing power whatsoever, anywhere.

"A governing constitution or *'Charter'* would specify that the Wealth and Industry of the Planet would belong to eve-

24

ryone, each according to his or her need, *Physical as well as Spiritual*. Each of these allotments would be made by the presentation of this new distribution device, called the *'Share Card'*.

"For the first time in all history, each of the many kinds of essential 'Industries' would be able to operate unrestricted by the control of 'Business' or any other 'Private interest'. Since there would be no need for Banking Institutions, Insurance Companies and etc., these would be disfranchised. The buildings, which they now occupy, could be converted, as necessary for other uses.

"As I have indicated, this 'New Economy' would provide for all of each person's present and future needs and comforts, as a legal right of the person's existence as an individual member of the Planet. It is quite probable that the many individuals and families, who are now enjoying a life style typical of our affluent society, would of necessity, be democratically persuaded to scale down their life-style so as to maintain a proper balance of 'Sharing' in this new sustainable, world economy.

"I believe that now is the time for me to introduce you to the ultimate quest of our journey. This quest would be the ultimate of all Social Organizations, that 'something new under the sun'.

-11-

'Vi-Tocracy'

"I have coined this new word to apply to an all-inclusive type of Regional as well as World government of all the People, co-operating and managing 'Industry' for the people's General welfare. This concept would function without discrimination, for individuals of all national origins, colour, religions and sex, working in compatibility and in co-operation with all of the Forces and Elements of Life, in a sustainably sharing manner. It is quite important that we should include 'Nature' in all of her many forms and environments, to share in the maintenance of our planet Earth. For this reason I chose the name *'Vi-Tocracy'*. In actual fact, this type of government would be a government of Science and Industry controlled by the active will of the people, for the welfare of all the people as well as the sustenance of Nature in its many varied forms.

"'Vi' of 'Vi-Tocracy' refers to all of the *natural elements and life forces.*

"Today's 'democracy' is based on a 'Party System' of government, functioning in a competitive, 'Free Enterprise' society. On the other hand, 'Vi-Tocracy', would for the first time ever, allow all of the people to exercise control of all aspects of their physical lives, having due consideration and respect for each other, as well as for those other thousands of members of our environment.

"In a 'Vi-Tocracy', Industries, not Businesses or Party Politics, would speak for the people, supplying their many needs, compatible with the elements and the forces of Nature. All Industries, whether producing 'Services' or producing 'Goods', would be managed either by qualified Engineers, Technicians, Designers, crafts people or other spe-

26

cialists in that particular field. Each of these industries of whatever nature would be controlled and operated by those qualifying individuals within that Industry.

"The ideal arrangement would be for these Industries to be located geographically where best suited to their particular type of production and distribution, to the consuming public, as well as to the environment.

"This type of government would be a distinct and viable alternative to our present-day method of 'Party Politics Democracy'. In this new arrangement, the *'Share Card'* would represent the 'Voice of the People', without the use of the now, ineffective and unreliable 'Party politics', Business-oriented system which controls our world today. The various governing bodies of this 'New Society' would be completely different from what we have today. Technologists, Health Scientists, Educationalists and Environmentalists would replace the Business Economists and Political Scientists in today's Government organizations.

"'Party Politics' would need to disappear completely as being redundant and even harmful to the health of society. The 'Party Politics' philosophy of government would have no place in a 'co-operative type of society', which this new era would have become. 'Party Politics' is related to a competitive form of society, which goes counter to the co-operative philosophy.

"There would eventually be no political boundaries between provinces, states, countries or nations.

"I see people living in 'Autonomous Neighbourhoods' responsible to both theirs and to the neighbouring 'Neighbourhoods'.

"Each of the Neighbourhoods would have its own representative government. Its duties, among other things, would be to record the wishes and needs of its people as well as to co-ordinate the fulfilment of those needs in the best cultural interest of everyone in that particular geographic area.

"Each neighbourhood would revamp its existing 'Shopping Centers' or establish new ones to suit the revised 'Industrial System' operating in each of the neighbourhoods.

27

Here, the individual's *'Share Card'* would be the only 'Medium of Exchange device' necessary to obtain any of the available goods or services requested. Each neighbourhood would be electronically linked with every other neighbourhood. This would produce a vast communications network; using the enhanced Technology and Engineering devices which we now have and which have proven useful.

-12-

Universal Charter

"From here on my 'Back Forty', I visualize this new Society, this *'Global Village', as* a world organization subscribing to one comprehensive constitution or 'Charter'. Within this 'Charter' the universal law of 'Caring and Sharing' ('Thou shalt love thy neighbour as thyself') would be able to operate freely for all of humanity. This 'Charter' would necessarily embrace all creeds, all *colours,* all cultures, both male and female, as well as our natural Environment in an unbiased, sustainable and sharing manner.

"Briefly stated, this 'Charter' would recognize the *Common Origin of all Life* as well as the necessity for these Life forms to Co-exist. Co-existence implies Co-operation and Sharing among Individuals, as well as the *respect for all other 'Life Forms'*, as being vital parts of Creation.

In the Beginning

"'Caring and sharing', in this new society, would begin with the birth of the infant.

"After due consideration to family planning (planning in relation to other members of the Human Family as well as to Nature), this new Embryonic Member of the human race, would be treated and respected as a special, precious, new little Neighbour, who is about to be born into a society of other human beings, as well as other life forms.

"This 'Embryonic Person' would, from the beginning, seek and expect to get loving support, not only from the parents, but also from the neighbourhood into which it is about to enter.

"This baby of tomorrow would probably be delivered in one of the many up-to-date, people-owned and operated 'Health Science Centers', Clinics or Maternity Hospitals.

"Each of these institutions would be properly staffed, with well-trained, professional people, nurses, doctors, technicians, etc., each dedicated to Caring and Sharing, as and when needed. Health care house calls in this new era could be available whenever and wherever needed with the same skill and efficiency as in a sterile hospital environment.

"Throughout the labour period as well as during the delivery, the male parent, if possible, would be encouraged to be present in the delivery room, along with the medical attendants. The spouse's presence would give loving support and assurance to the labouring spouse, (the future mother and the child).

"It is now universally recognized that each individual of any age seems to fare best when in caring contact with another individual. This is an indication that, *We are indeed, each other's life support system*.

"In general, since Health care is an essential part of the 'Care and Share' philosophy and practice and since the present day health costs are a burden on many who need any special care, it follows that thus being relieved of all financial burden, the recovery of the patient to complete health would be more certain. This freedom from financial concern would make it more possible for each of us to be able to enjoy and share Life to the fullest.

"The 'Health Science Centers' of the future would deal with research as well as the overall management of all of the branches of health, mental as well as physical, including Pharmaceutical, Dental, Optical, Hearing, etc. All phases of Holistic Medicine would also be included in order to cover each person's physical and emotional health needs.

"Adequately equipped and staffed ambulance services would be classed along with each of the many other pieces of equipment required for health care, diagnosis and treatment.

"For the proper care of individuals in this society of tomorrow, each person's medical record would be safely kept and made available for updating from time to time as needed, from birth throughout the person's life. On leaving the Health Center, the patient, or those in charge of the patient, would be kept informed of the latest findings in all aspects of preventive medicine. Periodically throughout the life of the individual, health and nutritional information would be freely published through the various unbiased media. This information would likely originate directly from a division of the 'Education System'. This would be in line with the basic principle of having the latest health care advice and services available to everyone throughout his or her lifetime. This would be a vital part of the 'rights' of the people of the world.

"There is an irrefutable principle of all Life that says: for better or for worse, our environment does have a direct effect on the health of every living creature, including Man.

"In this New Global Society, population growth control would be an important issue to be dealt with. This concern could be made known to the entire world through the use of the several people-managed, unbiased communication systems including radio, TV, press, etc.

"Although birth control of some sort would be considered necessary, abortion, except for certain, necessary medical reasons would not be permitted, except under controlled hospital conditions.

"I believe that Nature frequently has her own unique ways of handling these situations, when they reach the critical stage. I have noticed that the Lesbian and the Gay communities have received a great deal of attention of late. This may be one of these unique ways 'Nature' has of handling this population growth issue. The same reasoning could apply to the sometimes, natural infertility of either or both of the male and female partners. If this is so, then perhaps man's ingenuously contrived methods to overcome this problem in the lives of these couples are morally and biologically wrong and should not be tolerated.

"This may be another instance where Nature is cautioning mankind that it is not well to interfere with her *Natural*

Laws! It is quite possible in this 'Global Village of Vi-Tocracy', that this research, except in rare cases, would be halted and declared a crime against 'Human Survival'.

"Now, our new individual member of the human race has grown into little 'Personhood' and has learned most of the skills of *social, co-operative living* from his association with his natural family as well as from society at large. This person is now ready for a general, formal education, which would be mandatory and made available to suit the age and learning ability of each child.

"As in the Health and Welfare functions of this future society, the schools would be equipped with all of the 'state of the art' devices, supplies and educational methods deemed necessary. These up-to-date teaching methods and equipment would enable each individual pupil to receive a general as well as a specialized education and training to suit it as an individual, as well as a functioning member of 'Industry' and 'Society' at large.

"The teaching staff would certainly be made up of individuals who not only have the educational qualifications, but also an inherent desire to share their knowledge and skills with children of all ages who hunger and thirst for this knowledge. As in our society of yesteryear, Education would be considered to be of supreme importance in the social scheme and given number one priority.

-13-

Share Card Shopping

"Now, depending on the natural, inherited ability of the individual, our member of society is ready to go out into the world as a qualified, capable, caring, serving, sharing person. This person has learned that, unlike his ancestors before him, he would not require any form of money tokens, grudgingly tendered by Dad, Credit Cards or Cheque forms or bank accounts to enable him to *pay as you go* in his daily activities. In lieu of *cash*, or *credit cards,* he or she would be carrying this one all-purpose *'Share Card'*. This card made of a durable material and of convenient size, would be his or her sole means for the acquiring of any and all the goods and services necessary for 'Total Living', in Leisure, in Sickness and in Health.

"In this rebuilt society, our new member would notice that there has been a considerable change in our shops and our shopping centers. The plazas, the shopping malls and the corner stores would have all changed hands as well as operating methods. They would all have become publicly owned and operated outlet centers, designed and retrofitted to suit the products to be dispensed. There would be no price tags anywhere. The advertising posters advising the customer what brand to buy would all be missing. All of the food items displayed would be guaranteed fresh and wholesome. Nutritional information would be clearly noted making grocery shopping and meal planning more of a pleasure than a chore.

"All hardware items would be guaranteed to be as advertised and repairable or replaceable. Each item would be identified by a bar-code permanently attached to the article.

This bar-code would still be necessary for identification as well as for inventory accounting purposes.

"For the shopper there would still be the familiar checkout counter or desk. Here the checkout attendant would be required to pass the article through the regular scanning process. This would be followed by the customer exercising his or her 'democratic rights' with his or her 'Share Card'. This would probably be swiped through or scanned by an electronic gizmo in much the same manner as is now done with the 'Interac Card'. The information from these processes would be conveyed electronically, as a joint requisition, to the 'Manufacturing Industry' concerned with the production. This activity in effect, would ask the manufacturing industry to transfer and re-assign from the warehouse stock, the requested article or articles to the purchaser. Similar requisitions would go to primary industries and thence to the raw material source or sources, as well as the energy source or sources.

"This 'Share Card Way' is the way a 'Cashless' purchase of any nature, whether for natural or processed goods and services would be requested by the consumer in our new 'Global Village'. This is the way that an accurate material accounting could be kept of everything fabricated and dispensed from pins and needles to Jumbo Jets. This same reasoning would apply to services of any kind including Education, Health, Transportation, Recreation, etc., etc. The *'Share Card'* would represent the 'Demand' which would activate the 'Supply' from the appropriate source or sources.

"Yes indeed, all Industries would be operated and managed by people, Scientists, Engineers and Technologists who were qualified in their specialized field, along with managers and co-workers. These individuals, as members of Industry would all work co-operatively for the people, as requested by the use of this magical little *'Share Card'*.

"Managers of the Industry, of every level would be elected from within the Industrial organization, strictly on a merit basis. Demand and Supply, working in unison, would

34

serve to keep production active. This, in turn would keep people employed and happy at the kind of work they would be genetically and educationally qualified to perform. This would make it possible for every article or service to be unconditionally guaranteed for the life of that article.

"Because they do not have to follow the dictates of competition and the restrictive control of Business and its concern about profits to share-holders, these Managers of Industries would take greater pride in the products they produce. Note that I said 'Managers of Industry'. Many of those employed in businesses of the 'old regime' could probably find employment with some form of industry serving as 'Product Accountants', clerks, etc.

"Oh yes, conservation of world resources is mandatory for the ultimate survival of all Life. It is therefore very important that Manufacturers and Consumers unite to limit the Demand for Production and use of unnecessary things, devices or gadgets, which are now flooding our retail markets. In today's world, the main purpose for this multiplicity of unnecessary articles flooding our retail market seems to deal with Business's obsession with 'the gross national product'. This in today's market economy is considered vital. This co-operative action would in fact also help to prevent the drain on our depleting natural resources and at the same time help to reduce the general pollution of our environment.

"In the realm of Health and Welfare, this proposed *'Share Card'* would replace the now familiar 'Health Card'. As well as giving access to any and all the knowledge and skills available from the 'Health Sciences', this card would be a means of accessing the holder's health records to those who might have a legitimate need of this information, such as employment offices, etc.

"The card holder's *educational records* could also be made available for use in employment offices or wherever else they might be needed.

"As was previously stated, or inferred in the 'Charter', there would be the assumption that *this planet belongs to everyone* - not to any one corporation, or any one group of nations, or any one race or person. Private Lands, Forests, Waterways, Minerals, etc, would become public and as such, controlled and managed by and for the best interests of the public as well as the general ecologic welfare of the planet.

"Along with the *'Share Card'*, which everyone would be obliged to have and carry at all times as one now carries one's wallet, would go the obligation, in as far as one is physically able and qualified, to share in the work and any other activity required in producing those things and services which are generally asked for by the *'Share Card'*.

"Those individuals who are or who might become physically or mentally handicapped, in such a way that they could not qualify for any form of service, could be adequately cared for as would be required through the help of the Health Science Centers. No one needs to 'be left out in the cold', literally or figuratively, because of the lack of caring and sharing of the Planet's People and Resources

"The regional employment offices associated with each 'Industrial Complex' could be electronically or otherwise linked to the 'Health Services' as well as to the 'Education Services'. In this way full employment of capable, qualified, satisfied individuals, engaged in activities where they are best suited, would insure that there would be few if any labour management problems with which to deal.

"Handcraft industries and folk art would be encouraged as necessary for the fuller development of the individual. This activity would be classed in the realm of entertainment and fine arts, which could be further classified under the general heading of 'Education Services'. A practice and study of these 'Fine Arts' would all be deemed necessary for the development and understanding of our diversified World Cultures .

-14-

Drug Addiction

"Well Neighbour, I notice that you are not lighting up, so I guess you don't smoke. You don't even have a 'chaw' now and then? Good! I guess you too enjoy the clean fresh air.

"Good, I am with you on this. As a matter of fact I never have used that noxious weed in any form.

"For some time, these tobacco products have all been certified as being harmful to a person's personal health as well as to the health of the environment. Most of our health and environmental authorities are convinced of this glaring fact, yet very little is being done about it.

"The tobacco plant, as is well known, contains a very harmful and addictive drug Nicotine. This can, among other ways, be released as a by-product of burning. Apart from the labour of cultivating and harvesting the plant, the several products derived from this plant require very little hand labour to produce. The mark-up and hence the revenue to be made from the tobacco plant is considerable. Soil specialists tell me that the extensive growing of this plant deprives the soil of its usefulness for the growing of other more beneficial plants.

"Many mega-corporations as well as individuals and governments, currently reap vast fortunes from this health-destroying, addictive weed. Therefore little can be done as long as we allow this 'money incentive' to interfere with the health and wellbeing of humanity.

"In a cashless society, where money would have no value and things no price, it would be quite easy to completely ban the production and use of all tobacco products from society. The same would apply for the use of the several other habit-

37

forming, health-destroying products derived from plants such as cannabis, opium and their derivatives. With the disappearance of the 'money incentive', 'Drug Pushers' would likely disappear altogether from the crime scene.

"These 'drugs' are classified as drugs, which, in controlled conditions, may be useful in the pharmaceutical industry, for the benefit of the human race.

"Much the same can be said regarding the current widespread production and use of alcoholic beverages which are responsible for much of today's street and road crimes.

"When the profit value disappears along with the insatiable desire to 'have one for the road' (even when there is no road), the distillers and bottlers can turn their fabricating attention and skills to other uses in the field of chemistry. There are many beneficial uses for alcohol products as in the manufacture of fuels for clean energy production. This distilled plant product even now, finds its use in the many types of plastics products which are produced for a million or more uses in home and Industry.

-15-

Production Industries

"Over the centuries, in order to supply human needs, man has devised and constructed 'Production Industries' of numerous kinds. With man's ingenuity, these manufacturing plants have produced various things which have been deemed necessary for his well-being, livelihood and development. From the humble, versatile toothpick; food and clothing for the body; houses complete with furniture and electronic gadgetry; bolts, nuts and nails; to automobiles and supersonic jets, these and a million more things from the sub-microscopic to buildings reaching to the clouds are all things devised by the inventive mind of man and developed by 'Industry'. It is not always realized, that to produce each of these things, basically, 'Industries' require various forms and amounts of Energy, all supplied by Nature. Each of these industrial products is made by men and/or women who control this energy as it acts upon a variety of raw materials also supplied by Nature from planet Earth.

"This same scenario holds true for our many Service Industries - Health and welfare, Education, Transportation and Communication, Entertainment, etc. Each of these Industries also requires people who have trained themselves in different skills and qualification to operate these Industries so as to produce the service that it is designed to give.

"One might say that an 'Industry' begins with an idea or ideas. In order to materialize this idea, tools are required. In order to manipulate and operate the tools, people with a variety of skills and engineering ability, such as Scientists, Engineers, Technicians, Managers, Workers and Clerical staff are required.

"All of these groups are obliged to co-operate among themselves, and depending on the nature of the 'Industry', with other groups.

"It is assumed in today's world of 'Industry' that a non-productive activity which we call 'Business' is required in order to facilitate the distribution of these industrial products whether 'Goods' or 'Services', to the consuming public. For this reason, 'Business' and 'Industry' are usually twinned and intermixed. It is falsely assumed that neither one can exist without the other. This is partly true. If there were no 'Industry' there would be no need for 'Business'. However, the reverse does not hold true, because 'Industry' has existed in many instances without the help of 'Business'.

"These statements are meant to show that Industry of any form, type or size can exist without the help or interference of Business of any kind in performing its social function in the public interest, for as long as a need exists for this type of 'Goods' or 'Service'.

"It is generally true that Business exercises its control by establishing the 'Price' as well as the 'Quality and Quantity' of the Industry's products. This control tends to restrict the distribution of the product to only those who have the right amount of ready Cash or certifiable Credit to tender in exchange for the product, whether in the form of goods or service.

"Nowadays without this correct amount of cash or credit, regardless of urgency or need, none of these goods or services can be legally obtained. In many cases this produces tragic consequences, leading to the sorts of 'Crime', which are associated with the conditions of Poverty, Hunger, and Disease among groups of people in many parts of our lopsided world. This condition exists among adults as well as children who do not have this 'wherewithal' to obtain decent clothing, food and housing.

"So we have an increasing number of charity organizations begging for help for these 'Runners of the Human Race', our brothers, who cannot keep up.

40

"It may not be a commonly recognized fact that our familiar 'Money Price System' was indeed the invention of 'Business and Banking'. This System has been given the divinely sanctioned ability and 'right' to multiply itself in the hands of the astute and unscrupulous. This has now *given Business* and Profit almost *complete control of our Lives* and in turn of our Civilization.

"I hope to make it quite understandable that the products of Industry of all types could have been produced and distributed quite as efficiently without the help of Business in any form. I affirm this in spite of the fact that in today's world, it seems unquestionably necessary for 'Business' to enter the picture when it comes to distribution, sales and marketing on all levels. As a matter of fact, I believe in many instances, the general population has been very adversely affected because Business and Profit have exercised their assumed power of control.

"None of these adverse side effects on the consuming public could have occurred had the *'Share Card method'* of production and distribution been employed in any given transaction.

"As I have previously mentioned, when a purchase of any kind would take place, whether of goods or of services, communication in the form of an electronic requisition or *'Share Card'* would be established with the supplier of the finished product, to produce and supply the thing or service requested. This would set in motion, all the way back to the origin of raw materials, a series of internal requisitions. For this continuous flow of information to take place, the related industries would need to be electronically linked in a vast communications network.

"In many of our large industrial operations, there is already a network of a sort in operation. With some minor alterations this network as I described could quickly be made operable. When this is done, we could maintain a continuous balance between Production and Distribution as well as a continuous Employment of Personnel.

"I maintain this would produce a Distribution System that could adequately and fairly provide for the consuming needs of the World's population without the use of any kind of Business, or Money transaction.

-16-

Free Enterprise in Crisis

"At the dawn of this twenty-first century, we find ourselves caught, in a subservient civilization of Humanity. Here in the Western World, especially, we call this sort of civilization, 'Free Enterprise'. This civilization is dependent for its livelihood, however precarious, on a 'Money Price System'. As you know, this is the system that uses Money tokens, Cheques, Credit Cards or Bank Cards, *to be exchanged for one's livelihood* whether it is for food, clothing, shelter, health, recreation, communication or transportation.

"In this system, we find ourselves moving at an ever accelerating rate in order just to keep up. We have been conditioned to believe that it is not good enough to just keep up. In order to make sure, we constantly try to 'get ahead' by making some sort of investment stockpile or 'nest egg' for this future time when we can no longer work to 'earn a living'. In the meantime the gap between the Rich and the Destitute is continually widening.

"Climate change (Global Warming) seems to be increasing at an alarming rate and is threatening an increasingly devastated world. This in turn, increases the living hazards for both flora and fauna. Not only is our world being materially devastated; it is deteriorating socially and spiritually as well.

"Our responsible governments agree that it is necessary to do something about this 'Global Warming' crisis, as well as the associated social issues. These are all becoming more complicated with each passing day.

"Authorities tell us through the media that today is not the day to start *'that something'*. With many Big Business and Banking interests interfering with and influencing social action, they say it is politically expedient to wait until tomorrow! In the meantime the problems become more serious and tomorrow may, very well be too late.

"It is our responsibility, the responsibility of people everywhere, through the method of referendums, to decide to evolve from where we are in civilization, from the old, outdated monetary system to a true 'Cashless' system designed for the distribution of all goods and services. This can be done, if we wish to do it and if we have the political will to act out this wish.

"The cost would be minimal. The benefits would be maximal. This would become an international project; requiring international co-operation among all Nations and among all citizens. Furthermore, it would require no monetary funding and no taxes, personal or corporate to accomplish this changeover.

"I am not saying that we as individuals should stop doing 'our neighbourly bit' toward helping our Neighbour and our society. All of these things help considerably but temporarily to relieve some of the world's suffering. What I am saying and emphasizing is that until we start to do the 'drastic thing' towards revealing the real cause, the 'Grass Roots' cause of our 'Social Ills', then these ills will probably grow worse, becoming chronic and infectious.

"I believe that it is apparent that the media, the journalists and the politicians of any party, as well as the social benefit organizations, all regard this 'Money price System' as inviolate, untouchable and too sacred to criticize, let alone blame and pass judgement on. After all, I firmly believe, since Human Beings devised this system with all of its faults and modifications, why shouldn't we as other human beings, have the right to criticize and modify it to our liking?

-17-

"The Other Way"

"Must you leave now, Neighbour?

"You have a few cows to milk as well as the regular farm chores to do? Well Nature needs attending to as well, I suppose!

"While you are on the milking stool stripping that last drop of milk from your favourite Jersey, I hope that you will think on the things that I have told you! Perhaps you wouldn't mind getting on your party-line telephone, when you finish these chores, and tell the neighbourhood about the interesting time you have just had with 'Timothy Haystubble' as well as all of those interesting ideas of his. If you tell them in the strictest confidence, I am sure it will soon be broadcast neighbour to neighbour throughout the whole county!

"If you would be dropping by tomorrow, I promise to tell you more of this 'Vision'. I also promise you some more of this fresh, sweet 'apple cider'.

In the meantime remember this:

"A moving finger writes upon the ageless pages of Time:
'It is not our greed alone which is to blame for
the Sins of Society. Greed is just one of those several side
effects which result from the cause. This cause
I have already told you!

45

"Our *Centennial* project for the *New Millennium* now
becomes quite clear.
A New Age will not be aborning,
without the devoted assistance
of well trained *'Midwives'* to assist
in bringing into being this
New Age,
a *'Caring and Sharing Civilization'!*

"There is a 'Universal Principle' that makes all of mankind brothers. Not one of us ever does those things we think we do, all by ourselves. All that we do, all that we think and all that we say, in some way affects the lives of *all others* as well as our own. Yes, we are indeed 'Our Brother's keeper!'

By the same reasoning we are each other's
'Life support System'.

Now allow me to Show you a new Revelation:

"*When Mankind has spoken in Referendum, at the sound of a new Liberty Bell, the doors on all of the Wall Streets, and all of the Bay Streets of the world's Developed and Developing Nations, as well as the temple doors of the Moneychangers, everywhere would silently close. The power to their Computers and their Banking Machines would be switched off.*

This would be the signal for the
Final Crash!

*In some future time these doors may reopen to
Museums of Man's past,
And now
Forgiven Folly.*

The old earth along with the old ideas of Heaven
Would have passed away.
A new Earth- *a new era-with a universally attainable Heaven
would have arrived
for all of Humanity to enjoy, each to his or her own and together, as one Family of Mankind. Each man and each
woman could then sit and worship under his or her own
Fig Tree, each in his or her own way!*

*"To make this happen, we would each be doing a necessary
part when we begin to learn, even against the obstacles of
today's world, to Love all of our Neighbours.
It matters not our Culture, Religious Faith, Skin Colour, Racial Heritage, Social Status, Age or Sex,
The essential Christian social message
Was delivered to and for all of Humanity,
both Civilized and Primitive.*

*Here let me paraphrase
The Second Great Commandment:*

*"For the ultimate salvation
Of our human society,
It is necessary that we all strive
To work together,
Bearing one another's Burdens".*

-18-

Global Village

With this pattern, which I have drawn for you,
Let us now begin to fabricate that "New Wine Skin",
which has been designed to hold the
Sparkling "New Wine"
Of the 21ˢᵗ Century.

"Hi! A very good morning to you, Neighbour!
Thanks for dropping by!

"They say that it is a healthy exercise for one to visit with someone every day. This keeps one in daily contact as well as in 'daily caring for one's human kin'!

"We are fortunate this morning! I have just pressed a fresh pitcher of that refreshing apple cider for us to enjoy as we resume our little chat today!

"Just the other day, in my reading, I came across three related words and phrases. I expect that you have already seen and wondered about them? Well, in case you haven't here they are:

'Global village', 'Globalization', 'Global Domination'.

"These are the three popular catch phrases which appear quite frequently and cause quite a stir in the world-wide media.

"Ideally, 'Global Village' describes the nature, in the near future, of our civilization here on our planet, Earth.

"It is unfortunate however, that not all groups or individuals have the same visions of this 'Global Village' to which we are rapidly and surely travelling. Will it just happen, or do we, as individuals make it happen by those things that we do and the things we fail to do? Our various electronic communication systems (Radio, TV, the Computer with its Worldwide Network) along with the high speed and long range travel systems are daily bringing the various peoples of the world closer and closer together. These electronic devices are useful in allowing us to see and understand each other more clearly.

"Each of the many different interest groups, (thanks to free speech) has its own idea of how the unification of our civilization should look and function as a 'Global Village'.

"For the power-addicted 'World Politician', the 'Business Mogul' and the competing 'Banking Institutions', who are anxious to have control of the planet in the name of 'Big Business', it means that six billion people, for better or for worse, would eventually come under their control.

"If and when this should happen, the World Politicians, even under protest, would become 'Lackeys' to a 'Big Business plus Banking duo'. Under these conditions, the most successful World Politician would be the one who had learned to say 'Yes' to these Twins at the appropriate times.

"However, when this time should come, I am fearful that the rest of the world's population would lose all of the rights they ever had to a 'rule of democracy'. With these twins in control, I am afraid that the world's Natural Resources would soon be over-exploited and Global Pollution would increase to the point of disaster. Climate Change (Global Warming) would accelerate out of control. Consumerism would continue to grow and expand, nationally and internationally. Free Enterprise would undoubtedly increase, and getting out of hand, become 'Haphazard Enterprise'

"Wars have already taken on new meaning. The 'Magic Broomstick' has been broken into a thousand pieces. 'Global Terrorism', to some extent, has taken the place of the once dreaded possibility of 'World War III.' As we are talking, the 'Have' countries, represented by a coalition of super powers are 'waging all-out war' against an unseen and unknown enemy in an effort to combat this 'Global Terrorism'.

They hope to destroy the alleged 'Terrorists' nests, wherever they are, thus relieving the world of a 'Terrorist' threat.

"It seems that the 'world leaders' have yet to learn, from the two major world conflicts in the last century, that waging wars, no matter how seemingly justified, cannot end wars of any kind. Unfortunately, it seems that the *'eye for an eye'* culture is still active among us. This ancient philosophy *does naught but destroy our insight, our foresight and our hindsight.*

"In my own 'book of knowledge', I find that the quickest way to end anything destructive or annoying is to *just stop* doing the destructive and the annoying thing or things.

"The political leaders of these superior 'Christian' countries seemingly have not yet learned that the basic philosophy of all three major religions is to return **'Good for Evil'**, not 'Evil for Evil', as has been happening internationally, up until now.

"From my view here on my 'Back Forty', I wish to suggest that there surely must be enough intelligence among the leaders and their advisers of these 'Have' nations, to realize there must be a root cause for these 'Terrorist Cells' to have been formed in the first place. Furthermore, I believe that we ourselves are not completely blameless. It has been said, 'He who is without sin, let him cast that first stone!'

"I often wonder if our 'Civilization' could possibly have been built on the wrong foundation. Any sort of structure requires a proper base from which to build, if it is to function properly, indefinitely.

"Many millenniums ago bases were fabricated on which to build this Civilization which was supposed to survive until this millennium and far beyond. However, the sagging roof sections; the crumbling walls; the squeaky, uneven floors and the failing superstructure are all indications of a basic flaw in the design of these bases. It has been said, however, that the design for these bases was sanctified by Divine authority as being right and proper for the use of a Civilization that should last for Eternity. I wonder did those builders listen to the 'Proper Authority'.

"Several millenniums later, just two millenniums ago, the **'Correct Authority'** advised us that we had been 'duped'; the very foundation of our Civilization which we fondly refer to as *Christian* was incorrectly designed and built.

"He said in paraphrase, 'it is still not too late to change, to remodel, if you really wish to do so. However, this change has to be made completely and comprehensively'.

"Until now, while I am talking to you, no basic change has yet been attempted to this long-established method, which we have used, for the distribution of the fruits of our labours, to all of those members of our human family, on an equal and just basis.

" 'He', who advised us, is patiently waiting to hear from us in this regard!

"In today's world, these three units, *Banking, Business,* and *Politics* are inexorably bound together forming one *'Mega-Conglomerate.'*

"This 'conglomerate' forms the basis of our present 'Civilization' and will continue as such, for this 'Global Village' of tomorrow. This 'Mega-Conglomerate' will take over, unless we, the citizens of the Earth *speak out now*, loudly and clearly and at the same time act positively and firmly!

-19-

Industry

("The Superstructure for our World")

"From this view, here on my 'Back Forty', I can see that 'Industries' of all types, not 'Businesses', form the real superstructures of our world. Is this assumption not correct?

"Please do not interrupt me if I seem to repeat what I have already told you. I repeat because I believe that these ideas need repeating many times for our Neighbours to see and hear the truth as I have tried to reveal it to you.

What is Industry?

"For the purposes of this discussion, we could define Industry as that activity which takes place when one or more individuals decide to set about making an 'idea' come to life in the *service of mankind.* Having brought this 'idea' to life, it should then be made available to any and all of those folks who believe that they have a real need for this manifested 'idea'.

"At this point the 'industrialist', whether an individual or a group acting as a firm or company, has the option of either giving away the products of this realized 'idea', or exchanging them for something of equal value (barter).

"From Industry's primitive beginning back in the handcraft days until the uncertain present day, Industry has evolved through many stages of growth to the now semi-automatic, as well as automatic, mass producing factories of today. These factories are capable of producing even more than they can profitably distribute for consumption by today's consuming society.

"I believe we talked about this several days ago. Industries all start with an idea or several ideas, nurtured by a need of some sort. These ideas are usually combined with supporting ideas, assisted by the input from scientists, technicians, engineers, machinists, equipment operators, inspectors, forepersons and then some sort of Distribution Center or Warehouse. From here, the products are made available to qualifying customers. (Qualifying customers are those who are able to tender, either the right amount of cash or the equivalent in some form of certifiable Credit).

"'Business' entered our culture at about the same time as 'Industry' and growing apace in each other's companionship has lasted as an idea and as an institution until this present day.

"In today's world, 'Business' unites with 'Industry' for the purpose of controlling and distributing 'Industry's' products. For doing this service to 'Industry', a price is always expected which is called a mark-up or 'profit'. The more the accumulated profit, the more successful is the business. This is what 'buying low' and 'selling high' is all about. The greater the distance between these two, the more astute as a business person, one becomes.

"Although this may make 'winners' in the business world, one must remember that whenever there is a winner in any game, there is a loser right alongside. Morally, a loser is often a debt against society.

"Once into the race, the participants must keep running to the finish line or else drop out and 'declare bankruptcy'. To keep running means to keep growing and expanding. The prize at the end of the race is often called 'Big Business. This continuing contest among Big Businesses in time tends to produce a social environment of growing discontent, unrest, poverty, crime, violence, corruption, and ultimately warfare.

"These infractions of natural laws would result in the pollution and destruction of our 'man-made' as well as our Natural Environment.

"Yes, we have come a long way since that first business deal, whenever that was. Through many millenniums 'Business' has become a vital part of our culture, producing both good and bad consequences for the 'human race' as well as for our 'natural environment'. Do we not see the handwriting on the wall? It may be that we are a bit reluctant to admit to the errors generated by the practices of our 'business economy'. We are I believe, reluctant to admit that the 'Rule of Law' has reached the point where it can no longer work alongside Nature's 'Law of Justice' and 'Compassion'.

"I believe these notorious twins *Business and Banking Institutions* have long assumed that they were necessary for the birth, the operations, the control and growth of Industry. On the other hand, as I mentioned earlier in this discussion, I believe this active institution of Industry can function perfectly well, perhaps better, without the use of these, 'Business and Banking twins'. Let me hasten to say, an alternative method, designed to replace the use of money tokens or credit in any of their many forms, is not only necessary but is possible and even long overdue. To accompany this alternative to money, we require a special type of accounting system that would keep an accounting of the flow of Natural (raw) materials, through the various industrial processes to the consumer as a finished product.

"My invention was indeed conceived with this purpose in mind. Several of the functions now associated with Business would be required to work in partnership with Industry, namely: the accounting of raw materials in, versus the finished product going out.

"I believe that our immediate concern is to make sure that the realization of this 'Global Village' will be the outcome of what 'We the people need and want'. So let the people speak! Let the people vote in referendum, after all of the facts and consequences are revealed to them!

"I have no doubt that *'Globalization'* for *'Mega Business'* would mean expanded markets for their particular trade and commerce. 'Globalization', the building of the 'Global Village' in the interests of Business and Banking, would mean the growth and spread of Capitalism and the 'Competitive Spirit', as well as 'Free Enterprise'. This form of

'Globalization' means more money for *'Mega-Business'* with less and less for the 'Poverty-stricken majority, both here and in the 'Developing Countries'.

-20-

Global Survival

"To me this means the design and installation of a new and simpler type of society. This would be a society, having a 'State of the Art' built-in distribution system. This system would be designed to be able to accurately and fairly distribute to each person, as is required for his or her good, the products and services which our Science-enlightened and Technologically-equipped Society are able to produce. *This new society would operate in a completely and truly cashless manner.* It would include people of all racial origins, all cultures, all colours, and all religions, male and female, young and old.

"This Society, which I am describing to you, would be a world-wide society of people living in harmony with each other and with Nature. It would be self-governed with an all-embracing Charter of Rules and Principles.

"For the first time since the fabled 'Garden of Eden', mankind would be able to insure his co-operative 'Global Survival' along with the conservation of the natural world resources; the elimination of harmful pollution and the *securing of the probability of Peace and Fellowship among all* of the Inhabitants.

"My friend, I am aware that for several centuries, well-intentioned, concerned individuals have been engaged in philanthropic efforts to improve the conditions in their corner of society. They were no doubt spurred on by their faith, believing that even this little service they were doing was having an accumulative effect.

"At the same time, these well intentioned individuals and groups were being told by a so-called reliable source that

'Evil' and 'Sin' are necessary components of God's imperfect world and as such, must be tolerated.

"It seems to me, this concept is a direct 'slap in the face' to the 'Creator' of our universe. On the contrary, I believe 'evil' and 'sin' to be the result of man having digressed from following 'Nature's laws'. These laws have been formulated to insure the proper operation of our Universe.

"We are also assured that mankind can be forgiven with a chance to begin again, when he has been given a 'New Vision of Reality'. I believe that we are now discussing one phase of it. This 'New Beginning', is a matter of sufficient importance that I believe, it will bear repeating.

"In the Christian Bible, we can read these timeless Words of Wisdom, which I paraphrase as follows:

"After having paid my respects and devotion to God, my Creator, as well as to myself, God's unique creation, then I must regard and respect each and every person with whom I come into contact, with equal 'Regard', 'Appreciation' and 'Respect'.

To quote Edwin Markham:

> No one walks alone.
> All that we send into the lives of others,
> Comes back into our own.

"As individuals, we are eternally linked together by the invisible bonds of Spirit. At the present stage of our 'evolution', for our survival, we are obliged to work together among ourselves and with the rest of Nature, to share one another's burdens.

-21-

Global Village
"The Other Way"

"Based on the forgoing precepts, with the guidance of that helpful 'Still Small Voice', whispering to me here on my 'Back Forty', I received the instructions for the building of this 'New Wine skin', which when realized would become the beginning of a *'Care and Share Society'*.

"Today's world of some six billion people is, at present, roughly divided into groups of people which we call Nations or Tribes. Each of these groups is usually characterized by having a distinct racial origin and culture. Each of these six billion or so people in these several hundred nations, live and work in what we refer to as cities, towns, and villages. Then there are several large areas, which we have grudgingly set aside to accommodate all of those other billions of lesser, though very important, Life Forms, which we collectively refer to as 'wild life' or Nature.

"Generally speaking, these 'natural areas' are assumed to be the responsibilities of the countries or nations who have claimed them, to exploit as they see fit. At present there seems to be no deliberate, political coordination among any of these various units as there should be for their wellbeing as well as ours.

"Each of the Cities, Towns, Villages, etc, in these nations, has acquired a name by which it is now known. These names have become an essential part of our geography and our heritage. In my plan, for political reasons, I have designated each one, or several of these units grouped together as a 'Neighbourhood'. Each 'Neighbourhood' would have equal status, politically with its neighbour and would be located on the world map by two co-ordinate numbers, Latitude and Longitude.

"Each 'Neighbourhood' would be politically autonomous, having its own Legislative Government elected by the people in much the same way as is done now, but devoid of all political party or other affiliations and influence. The existing municipal building, or buildings, would probably remain, but with changed functions.

"Each Neighbourhood would be responsible for the staffing and the maintenance of its Education Center, Culture Center, Health Center (Health Sciences Center), Recreation Center, Maintenance Center (including fire and police protection) as well as Administration (including Law and Order). The several types of non-competing Industrial Plants would of course dominate each Neighbourhood, in strategic locations to suit the type of industry and the ecology. Each functional unit would be staffed by qualified persons to suit the nature of the function that it would perform; but never by politicians or persons of prestige, seeking to attain some higher social status.

"The 'Executive Council' would consist of an official along with a deputy from each of the Industrial Groups as well as an official from each of the 'service centers' (Health, Education, Transportation, etc.). In other words, each member on the Executive Council would also be a knowledgeable, functioning member of the Neighbourhood.

"The Legislative Bodies from each of the Neighbourhoods would be electronically linked, in such a way that one Neighbourhood could share information with any other Neighbourhood when a need arose. This arrangement makes it possible for each area, each continent and eventually, the entire Planet to be linked in a co-operative network of **'caring and sharing'**, operated and controlled by each citizen as he or she uses the plastic *'Share Card'*.

"Does this sound a bit fantastic?

"Would this concept be too good to ever be true?

"As long as we look at it that way, it probably will be just an impossible wish, unfulfilled. If we can see it as 'do-able', then it could become a fulfilment when its time has come. This time of fulfilment is up to each of us working co-operatively for that one common goal.

-22-

Charter

*The words **'Caring and Sharing'** would form the 'Crown' or 'capstone' of a new constitution which would become the charter of all the people, and known as*
'CHARTER'.

"This certified document would contain all of the governing principles necessary to co-ordinate and control the six billion and growing members of the human race, as well as their relationship to Nature.

"In this manner, from the 'Grass Roots', the people of the world – all Nations, all Colours, all Religious beliefs, Male and Female, could co-operatively share in this great plan to rescue the people of our Planet along with their natural environment, from that pending catastrophe which has been prophesied by both the Scientific world as well as by certain religious groups.

"This 'Preamble' sets forth the basic, Universal Beliefs and assumptions on which the 'Charter' would be based. These could be known as:

The Words

"Our world is but an infinitely small bit of an *infinitely large Universe,* which was created and is continuously being recreated by an *'All-Powerful',* mysterious, invisible, mathematically undetectable, yet intelligent *'Force',* which we will never fully know or even fully understand.

"This 'FORCE' or Power is believed to be a vital, integral part of all Life and not some exclusive, far off, high up, untouchable 'Potentate'. This **'IT'** has been given a number

61

of intimate, names such as: God, Jehovah, Allah, Almighty One, Our Heavenly Father, Creator, Great Spirit, etc. This all-powerful, creative 'Force' operates through each of us, even though we do not understand it, as our **'Consciousness'**, our **'I AM'**.

"We further believe that along with the material creation of the Universe, a complete set of physical and Spiritual laws, including the operating instructions was created and assigned to our keeping. We are expected to try to learn and understand these Laws. They control and govern all of Creation, the parts that we know and the parts, we may forever, know only in part. These 'Laws' are resolute without regard for the individual's 'Faith' or 'Religious Beliefs'.

"The 'Laws' with which we are the most familiar are the Physical Laws. We refer to these as the 'Laws of Physics', the 'Laws of Chemistry, the 'Laws of Biology, the 'Laws of Mathematics, etc. However, a discussion of these laws is not within the scope of our present discussion. Those have already been discussed in many treatises now filling libraries and academies around the world.

-23-

The Laws of Life

"The 'Spiritual Laws' in practice, are 'Ethical Laws'. They control our relationship to each other as well as to other 'Life Forms' (Nature) alive in the Universe. Ethical Laws become 'Moral Laws' when they find a place in our culture.

"The first of these two laws, we recognize as 'The Law of Competition', commonly known as 'The Survival of the Fittest'. It is probable that our idea of 'Free Enterprise' receives justification from this law. This law was valid when Life in its initial stages was being developed. Since Mankind has evolved to its present stage, it is seen that the *First Law,* in most cases could no longer apply. For this reason it is said the Creator established the *'Law of Co-operation'.* Henceforth, this law was expected to supersede that other version of 'First Law' in dealing with most matters of human relationships.

"Stated in the terms familiar to most, this 'Law of Co-operation' is worded thus:

'Thou shalt love thy neighbour as thyself'.

"In the course of time, it was discovered that co-operation among Human Beings seemed more effective when they felt more confident in themselves and had developed a sense of self-respect or self-worth. So in the course of time, the law of Competition was somewhat modified so that males and females alike, could learn to compete with themselves, not against each other, in order to achieve this sense of self-respect and self-improvement.

"This first law is now written in the Book of Life and translates as follows:

'The First Law of Life'

"We should each learn to honour and respect each of these inner, Spiritual Qualities of Kindness, Gentleness, Forgiveness, etc. as well as the love of the Beauty expressed in the Sights, Sounds and Feelings in Nature.

This should lead to self-improvement, making each of us better able to contact that 'Essence of God' within each of God's creation.

This 'Law of life' has been proven to have direct Physical Benefits as well.

'The Second Law of Life'

"We need to learn the truth that, indeed 'We are each other's Life Support System' and therefore are needed for each other's well being.

"It does not hurt to repeat: 'We are our brother's keeper'.

"In order to survive as a human species and to help create harmony in society, as well as to save and protect our environment,

We must all work together.

"Sustained under this umbrella-like 'Preamble' the political design for a new society in the 'Global Village' would germinate and grow. From here also would originate all the rules and regulations governing the inhabitants of the new 'Global Village' (the laws of the land).

-24-

The Global Village
of the 21st Century

"The Global Village of the 21st Century could be described as a World Federation of peoples, Cultures, and Nationalities, with its beginning at the grass roots level.

"This is the way I see it from the 'Back Forty'!

"Now imagine if you can our earth, the Globe, mapped out in a series of 'Neighbourhoods' interconnected as a part of a communication network. These 'neighbourhoods' would comprise one or several villages, towns or cities, and even 'wild life' areas. Each of these populated 'Neighbourhoods' would be politically autonomous.

"Now imagine several of these 'Neighbourhoods', cooperatively forming what could be called 'Neighbourhood Federations'. All of these Neighbourhood governing administrations forming the various 'Federations' would, be tied into this communications network. A number of these 'Federations' could then group together to form 'Regional Federations'. These also would be electronically linked with this global network. Going another step, when regional federations unite, we arrive at what could be termed 'Greater Federations'. The 'Administrations', as applying to each of the federations as well as to each 'Neighbourhood', would consist of various departments designed to serve each of the several functions necessary to serve the geographical as well as the ecological needs of the area. Each of these functional departments would be administered by a 'Committee'. The members of each committee would be academically qualified for that particular department, such as: *Education, Health Care, Industry, Communication, Transportation,* etc. Each of these committees would be chaired by a qualified Chairperson, appointed annually from within the department. In a similar manner each 'Neighbourhood' as well as each 'Federation' would be controlled by a Committee with its Chairperson who would be newly appointed every four years. These various federation 'Chairpersons' would constitute the Council of that particular 'Federation'.

"Finally, a 'World Federation' would be formed with representatives from all of the 'Greater Federations'. This would be the pinnacle of a 'world-governing pyramid'. In each case, on all levels, the elected 'Governing' personnel would need to be thoroughly technically qualified in the various technical arts and sciences of Industry, as well as conversant with the meaning and interpretation of the Charter.

"The members of this 'World Federation' would be required to appoint from within their ranks a governing body or 'Committee' with its chairperson and a deputy to serve a period of four years, not reappointable. This would be known as 'Global Council'.

"A Secretariat and staff of qualified personnel would be required, appointed from the council membership. The responsibilities of this Secretarial Office would be to record the deliberations of the 'Council' meetings and to insure that the whole world knows and understands the meaning of these deliberations. These reports would need to be made in a language or languages understandable to everyone, worldwide.

"It would be mandatory for the 'Global Council' in all of its deliberations, to subscribe to both the spirit and the letter of 'The Word' as it would be clearly set down and explained in the 'Charter'.

"One of the many immediate duties of this 'Global Council' would be to ratify the *'Charter' and its 'Preamble'*. Then, as soon as possible it should ratify the removal of all legal National boundaries that now separate nation from nation and state from state. When this is accomplished, one vast community of Neighbourhoods would result, sharing among themselves for the common good as well as each individual's good, as prescribed by the 'Charter'.

"This 'Global Council' would, through its number of well-staffed offices, situated throughout the world, be responsible for the coordination and co-operation of the many subordinate organizations (Neighbourhoods) on the planet. Furthermore, the 'Council's' duty would be to interpret and implement the information gathered from the various parts of the globe in order to verify that all production and distribution, with due regard to the forces and products of Nature would form a continually balanced equation.

"It is necessary that this 'Global Council' also keep a global inventory of the Earth's natural resources such as Mineral Products, Forest Products, Marine Products and Topsoil etc.; as well as the many products made from these raw materials.

"The responsibility of this Global Council would be to provide an overall global control of the uses and the distribution of these natural products, as well as to decide when to prohibit or ration their uses.

"The necessary data for this 'Global Products Accounting' would be supplied by each of the Neighbourhood accounting departments. When and where required, these Neighbourhood Accounting departments would also be required in decision-making.

"The pinnacle of this 'Governing Pyramid' would be represented by this Global Council, with the flow of information coming in balancing the instructions, in the form of 'orders' going out.

"The base of the pyramid is represented by those countless diversified 'Neighbourhoods', composed of citizens of the world. These people are in fact, the rightful 'shareholders' of this corporation, planet Earth. From this base, reports concerning the use of our natural resources as well as products and services dispensed to the population by means of the 'Share Card', would be communicated by the world-wide network. From this base, each of the times the 'Share Card' is used, the voices of the people would be having their share in a real way, in all matters concerning their welfare as well as the welfare of the planet.

"In this 'New Global Village', the people-approved 'Charter', manifesting through various levels of governing bodies, Councils and Committees, etc, would represent the controlling authority. There would be no need for any 'authoritative figure' which, as has been demonstrated many times in past history, could easily tend toward aggressive dictatorship. Figureheads as such as Prime Ministers, Presidents, Kings, Emperors, or other potentates, would become elements of history marking the steps of Mankind's march towards self-mastery.

-25-

Real Economy

"The inestimable wealth of this new Social System would not be measured in *gold* or *silver bullion* or with stocks and bonds. It would not be measured in Skyscrapers, Mansions or Castles. It would not be measured in Large Armies of massive, High-Tech, and destructive Fighting machines. In the place of all these popular status symbols, the Real Economy of this Global Village would be measured by the limitless potential of Human Worth coupled with the Earth's Natural Resources converted into Artefacts and Services for the welfare of every living being--Plant, Animal and Human.

"The 'Real Economy', in this proposed 'Share Card' society, could be distributed to every person according to a requested need for the sustenance and enhancement of his or her self, simply by the employment of this 'Share Card'. Each and every person as well as every organization would possess a suitable, authorized version of this simple yet valuable wallet-sized device, which would be used for the purpose of securing his, her or its justified portion of the Earth's economy. This small, simple yet valuable little device, used by people, social organizations and industrial organizations could maintain and keep 'civilization', its people and the environment alive, virile, productive and strong.

"As you can gather from the foregoing discussion, 'Industries' of many sorts, play a major role in both Today's and in Tomorrow's World. In the society of tomorrow 'Industry' would serve both as *Producer* and *Distributor, (from Producer direct to Consumer).* What an ideal arrangement for an efficiently operating Society!

"Most persons now occupied in the 'Business world,' would undoubtedly be able to find his or her ideal, congenial occupation, according to qualification, in one of the many 'Industries' to which he or she could be relocated.

"With both of these existing restrictions and handicaps ('Business' and 'Banking') removed, the actual operators of 'Industry' would soon naturally take greater pride in their share of the products and services produced. This would result in the voluntary conservation of the products of raw materials, eventually leading to a reduction of pollution and waste.

"The most significant of the beneficial changes could be found in Public and Private Health Care. Health Care applies to all 'Life', as I have previously stated, not just to our personal lives but also to those other living creatures around us. 'Health Care' also involves the use of many industries and activities, from metal working to electrical work, from pharmaceutical to food processing, optical, audio and more.

"Our individual health care involves our total environment, public utilities, the men and women on the street with and without special skills, medical doctors, specialists, nurses, and more. Health care is concerned with Education, special training and research as well as an appreciation of the mystery of Life and Creation around us. Health Care, as with other social services, requires '*Caring and Sharing*'.

"In today's 'civilized world', the activities involved in maintaining health for one's physical body, require money in increasing amounts as our civilization runs on, growing in monetary strength and physical deterioration. This simple fact makes it very difficult, many times impossible, for many people to maintain healthy bodies, as well as to heal the diseased or broken body.

"Apparently uncontrollable disease epidemics are now raging out of control because of lack of money to pay for the cost of drugs, hygienic living environment, medical research, doctors, nurses and other health services. This is happening in many parts of the world in both the developing as well as in the developed countries.

"We must remember that all of these unfortunate, sick and broken people, wherever they are, are also our Neighbours, in need of the caring and sharing from the rest of us.

"'Health Care' is just one of the several areas of our Society where the 'Money Price System' has very badly failed Humanity.

"In an enlightened, caring world, with this new 'Share Card' method of distribution, I am sure that these many cases of 'short change' to our Health Care System as well as other social activities would likely not have occurred.

"In this 'Caring Sharing' world of tomorrow, lacking the high-pressure sales promotional work which is associated with most 'Businesses', I notice that there would be a substantial reduction in the production of 'Things' (unnecessary things, gadgets and widgets). These are the things, which are now being produced, to eventually fill our scrap bins and our landfill sites.

"I foresee fewer motor cars being made and distributed, resulting in somewhat less highway and street traffic and therefore fewer accidents. I predict speed limiting devices required on all domestic road vehicles, whether new or old, with the exception of some emergency service vehicles.

"I see people of all walks of life moving at a much more leisurely pace, with seldom any compelling reason to be in a hurry. I see folks walking more and running less with an improvement in physical health. The character lines on people's faces are changing from frowns and worry to smiles and genuine laughter. This is making their days, your days and my days actually brighter.

"Among this stabilized population, I see not only happier faces, but more shoulder to shoulder rubbing, as well as more back slapping and less 'back-biting'. I see more 'chit chatting', leading to that long lost and almost forgotten art of street corner visiting, which has become popular again.

"All of this will have resulted in fewer work-place accidents as well as healthier, happier people living in this now happier, healthier world.

"However, let neither of us become too complacent. As the trends continue today, I can see the probability of a world Economic Crisis looming. This could happen early in this twenty-first century.

"I believe that we should take this probability seriously and be prepared to cope with a break-down of our Civilization along with the destruction of the Ecology. There are many things that we can all do together in order to help ease the impact of this impending 'Crash'.

"Think about what a little 'Caring and Sharing' Neighbour with Neighbour can do, now as well as in cases of Emergency.

"Every day, it is being revealed to more and more people that our civilization depends on the proper functioning of a 'Medium of Exchange' as well as the continuous functioning of our 'Industrial Establishments' to insure that people are kept busy, healthy and happy with an accompanying sense of security.

"It is more evident every day that our present 'medium of exchange' is indeed in acute trouble. Our 'Industrial Establishments', dependent as they are on the Business-oriented 'Money Price System', are likewise in dire trouble. Our political systems on both sides of the ropes are in a state of utter chaos."I believe that every day more and more people are questioning the meaning of '*things as they are*'.

-26-

Finale

"I am quite sure we do not wish for another *Joseph Stalin*, another *Kaiser Bill*, or another *Adolf Hitler*, or even *'Big Brother Business'* to assume control with the intent of offering to bail us out and so keep us from sinking. The present day political assumption that, *'Their good is also our Good'*, needs to be questioned and indeed revised.

"The task of running this world politically is too great an undertaking for any one person or any regime, of any stature, to undertake. Make no mistake about it. This task is one that requires the *co-operative efforts* of the total population working and sharing together, as I have outlined to you on our several previous little visits.

"There should be no doubt that mankind can succeed in making this detour to 'The Other Way'! Think about the huge engineering projects that have already and still are being successfully undertaken with intelligent co-operation. Among many others, I am reminded of man's attempts at trying to conquer space and his success of walking on the moon. What about his future plans in regard to Space travel? Then I am reminded of those architectural giants of glass and steel, the World Trade Center Towers, which took over four years of planning and construction to build but were destroyed in a matter of minutes, by a small handful of fanatics in a spirit of revenge, using two stolen American-built aircraft filled with hundreds of innocent human beings. Does this not illustrate that the sons of men can use their genius to destroy as well as to build when it suits their purpose?

"Here from my view at the Back Forty, I would like to suggest that these Twin Towers as well as the entire Financial District were originally built on the wrong type of

73

'Foundation'. It is to be hoped that the men and women of Manhattan would not subscribe to any idea of having these buildings replaced by the Business World on the same 'foundations', to serve their original purposes. 'Grass Roots' reasoning suggests that this same number of dollars would be better invested in improving the 'Back Yards' of Greater New York City, as well as the many other 'Back Yards' throughout our 'Developed' world.

"Why not start this rebuilding now while we still have the natural raw materials as well as capable, trainable sons and daughters of men and women to do these jobs? This, I believe, would present a much better gesture of brotherhood to the rest of our suffering planet than by showing off our 'power' and 'wealth' represented by 'Cash Flow' as would be signified by many other towers of glass, steel and concrete reaching into the sky. Are they trying to appease the gods, or are they saying, 'Look, we are Gods'?

"How much easier and more satisfactory it would be to construct a 'New Jerusalem', a place for all traditional faiths to enjoy; or a 'New Garden of Eden' in which all of Nature can flourish. How much easier it would be to make flowers bloom in the desert or to institute a *'Share Card Society'* using the foregoing plans which I have provided, on a well-constructed foundation of Fellowship and Goodwill.

"This well-tested foundation could be made to evolve from the present laissez-faire, monetary systems, (we all know so well). It could be gleaned from present day science and technology which gave us the Computer Age. This is the scheme which could be called the very ultimate of the *'credit card systems'*, designed for the distribution of all Goods and Services along with a world-coordinated political system especially designed for it to function.

"This method, which uses neither Cash nor Credit of the usual kind, I have called the 'Share Card Way', which is 'The Other Way'.

I repeat:
'Those who have ears to hear,
Let them hear and those who have eyes to see,
Let them see. The message
*Is on the **airwaves**;*
The handwriting is on the wall.

"Everything I have told you about and more could be realized by the use of this relatively simple 'Share Card' Distribution System, when operated by People, in the name of all the people, to control those vital, controllable functions of our society."

Until now, my visiting neighbour had listened attentively, apparently understanding and enjoying the portent of what I was most anxious to say to the World.

We both sat in silence for a time, enjoying the late summer afternoon. Then he spoke with the question I was anxious to hear:

"How can we realize this return to 'The Garden of Eden', this 'Utopia' you have been telling me about?"

I replied in the following manner:

"As I have explained several times, everything begins with an idea. This Idea has to be made known to at least a small group of 'sympathetic', intelligent folk who are in a mutual agreement that something fundamental needs to be done. Hopefully, after a little persuasion, it would be agreed that this idea should be studied, mulled over and developed in more detail.

"At this point, it would probably be agreed to form a non-profit, membership organization, having in mind the basic idea that this organization – not a Political Party – would grow to National and International significance. Then, when the time seemed right (*when the iron is hot*), National Referendums, followed by an International Referendum should be proposed, to give the whole World a chance to say **"YES"** or to say "NO" to this idea of evolving from this long over-due, redundant "Money Price System" to...

'The Other Way'—'the Share Card Way'

Appendix

Be it known, there are Eight Things that "Humanity" must learn to do in order to keep his species alive before that last tree in the rain forest has fallen and the last stream has ceased to flow. These are:

Phase-out the Ages-old "Money Price System" as a means of Exchange for a needed share of the world's supply of food, clothing, housing, etc.

Phase-out "Business" as a method for the distribution of those things, which are vital for the maintenance of life, health, creativity and growth.

Phase-out "Party Politics" which is an unjust form of control over the minority who are now struggling to be heard.

Phase-out the need for Competitive Aggression among people who are *different.*

Phase-in "Nature's way" of "Caring and Sharing" applied to the distribution of those things necessary for health-giving life and growth.

Phase-in "Industry's Way" for the production and distribution of Industry's products direct from processor (Producer) to consumer, giving to each according to his or her requested need.

Phase-out that outworn, hackneyed, aggressive type of association among all of life's species. This attitude produces distrust and fear, even hatred, war and destruction, among these beings.

Phase-in "Caring and Sharing" using the "Share Card System" for sharing the wealth and the needs of our Neighbourhoods and our Environment, thus providing the conditions necessary for the seeds of *"Peace and Goodwill"* to grow and flourish.

"Here is the Long and the Short of it"

Take one handful of miracles from the 20th century along with a small pinch of creative imagination!

Borrow the "galena crystal" from the "crystal detector" on your granddad's primitive radio which is now gathering dust in the attic. Add on a "semi-conductor" or two, which you will find lying around loose somewhere. Take a handful of clean washed, white sand and fuse it under the white heat of Nature's Laboratory. Add this new "Silicone Chip", thus created, to the three other miracles you are holding and unite them to form an "integrated circuit". Behold, now you have the components of the first "Personal Computer". You have now opened the "Pandora's Box", releasing the "Electronics Age" to the whim of a new generation of creative entrepreneurs, who were born with the genius for aggressive Big Business. These newcomers to the electronics science of the "Computers" would soon take over the whole field of Communications, along with Online Banking and a host of other now familiar miscellaneous gadgets, which are supposed to make living easier and faster.

With this small group of basic electronic units, a whole new world is being reborn. Some folks even dared to speculate about the idea of a "Cashless Society" evolving from an extension of the increasingly popular "Credit Card" idea.

In reality we have this handful of "electronic units", once again waiting to be coordinated and controlled for the benefit of Mankind!

This can all happen when we decide to adopt a special, general-purpose "Credit-debit Card", which fittingly could be known to the world as, **"The Share Card".**

"This, my Neighbour, is 'The Long and the Short' of a viable solution to today's Economic and Social problems.

78

Although this may sound *'a way out'*; even so, with a little thought, I think that you will agree that this *'way out'* could be '**The Other Way**' for Mankind to travel in order to avoid the many hazards we encounter on this present, troublesome and dangerous "Old Way".

  "**For Radical Results, we must learn to apply Radical Solutions.**

"I hear 'Urgent Voices' of those crying out across this
Wilderness of Civilization.
There is a Grand old World
Anxiously waiting to be renewed!
There are Billions of Hungry, Naked People asking to be fed
and clothed!
There are so many things
Waiting for a United, Co-operating,
Caring World to do."

Many Intelligent Men and Women have developed the Science and the Technology.
Nature has provided the Resources, (not limitless, but adequate for these tasks, if we use them wisely).
Let us get busy and do these jobs now
While we have the necessary Time
As well as the required materials.

It has been said, 'we are all in this game together'.

The ball has now been tossed for you to catch!

Thank you for patiently listening to my story.
I always enjoy sharing these ideas with all who may be
dropping by! If you wish to hear more,
You will find me here as usual, on the front stoop of my little
cabin, here among 'The grass roots of our Civilization',
Whittling and Meditating.
Do come again -
And bring your Neighbours!

Timothy Haystubble
(Back Forty)

Acknowledgements

There has been a large quantity of reliable, scientific source material published on the general subject of Ecology as well as statistical material on the progress and effects of Climate Change (Global warming). The exploitation and unnecessary waste of Nature's resources, both plant and animal have been well documented by reliable professionals and scholars in the field of Nature Conservation. I commend, without any hesitation, the research and educational work done by the David Suzuki Foundation in regard to Global Warming as well as the general subjects pertaining to the earth's ecology.

Going farther back to the early part of the last century and the great Depression of the thirties, I can cite the dedicated research work and writing of the late Robert B Langan of Chicago, Illinois.

The valuable contribution in the fields of the Arts and Sciences by the team of Walter and Lao Russell of Swannanoa, founders of the University of Science and Philosophy, Waynesboro, Virginia, must not be forgotten. There are many other individuals as well as organizations too numerous to narrate here, that have and still are contributing to the ideas of a necessary, radical Social Change aimed at rebuilding and enhancing the Human Society.

For further insights,
I invite the reader to drop in for a visit
with *Timothy Haystubble* on his web pages for more discussions of his "Views from the Back Forty" concerning topical, social issues.
(http//members.rogers.com/mumak/)

I invite your comments:
(Email - mumak@rogers.com)

Ken Muma
(Author)

July 15, 2002